THE LIFE & TIMES OF
JOHN F. KENNEDY

THE LIFE & TIMES OF

John F. Kennedy

BY
James Brown

This edition printed for, Shooting Star Press Inc, 230
Fifth Avenue, Suite 1212, New York, NY 10001

Shooting Star Press books are available at special discount
for bulk purchases for sales promotions, premiums, fund-
raising or educational use. Special editions or book
excerpts can also be created to specification. For details
contact – Special Sales Director, Shooting Star Press Inc.,
230 Fifth Avenue, Suite 1212, New York, NY 10001

This edition first published by Parragon Books
Produced by Magpie Books Ltd, 7 Kensington Church
Court, London W8 4SP
Copyright © Parragon Book Service Ltd 1994
Cover picture & illustrations courtesy of: The Mary Evans
Picture Library; Rex Features; Associated Press.

ISBN 1 57335 037 0
A copy of the British Library Cataloguing in Publication
Data is available from the British Library.

Typeset by Hewer Text Composition Services, Edinburgh
Printed in Singapore by Printlink International Co.

THE KENNEDYS

The USA is said to be classless society. But try telling that to the Kennedys of Massachusetts back at the turn of the century. From where they stood, as the descendants of Irish immigrants, largely confined in their earliest generations in the States to menial jobs, and exposed to prejudice and suspicion about their culture and about their Catholicism, power and privilege was firmly in the hands of the so-called Boston Brahmins. These were mostly WASPs – white Anglo-Saxon Protestants. Their sons received an elite education at the Ivy League universities. Many of them could confidently expect to go on to positions of prestige and power, buoyed up by family connections, inherited wealth and entrenched prejudice. Or so it looked to those, like the Kennedys, who felt themselves locked out of the charmed circle. In their determination to break into it, the Kennedys would eventually send one of their number, John F. Kennedy, to the White House; though, ironically, his candidacy for successive political posts would be backed by his vast inherited wealth, by the Ivy League education and contacts that wealth had brought him, and by all the string-pulling his awesomely powerful family could command. Encountering prejudice, the family's first response was not to fight injustice as such, but to make themselves so powerful that they would have nothing to fear.

Patrick Kennedy took his leave of Dunganstown in his native Ireland in 1848. He was twenty-five. His famine-stricken homeland was ruled, or rather misruled, by the British.

He fetched up in Boston, married a fellow immigrant, fathered five children, and in 1858 expired in an outbreak of cholera.

His youngest son, P.J., clawed his way out of poverty. He quit school, worked all hours and hustled. By the time he was twenty-five he owned his own saloon. Other businesses soon followed, and he went into Massachusetts State politics. Success and perfect rectitude didn't always go together. One of his eldest son's earliest memories was of two sidekicks turning up on the day of an election and announcing proudly 'Pat, we voted 128 times today'.

P.J. had done reasonably well. His eldest son, Joseph P. Kennedy (names put round that way to seem less blatantly Irish), was to do spectacularly. He went to Harvard University – home of the elite. He fared reasonably, but never quite felt he was accepted – partly, one suspects, because he did not really want to be. He wasn't going to fit in; he was going to be himself – aggressive, vulgar . . . and too rich to have to care.

Joe came down from Harvard in 1912. He embarked on a business career that was to bring him millions, though sometimes by questionable means. He went into banking (at the top, of course, as a bank president),

and thence into countless other interests —
Hollywood, the stock-market, wherever
there was a buck to be made. Or rather,
several million bucks to be made. His famous
son called him a financial genius; his critics
called him a swindler. One point is beyond
dispute: he became immensely rich.

The Founder, as he was sometimes known,
married Rose Fitzgerald, the daughter of
another Irish Boston politician, 'Honey
Fitz'. He cherished great ambitions for the
Kennedys. However, while as passionately
devoted to the advancement of his family in
the new world as any dynastic prince in the
old, Joe Kennedy was not greatly blessed
with, or did not care to cultivate, the virtues
of family life. He proved a promiscuously
unfaithful husband. The Kennedys were to
be great before they were good.

Rose Kennedy consoled herself with the rites and observances of the Catholic faith, and bore her husband nine children: Joseph Patrick junior (1915), John Fitzgerald (1917), Rosemary (1918), Kathleen (1920), Patricia (1924), Robert (1925), Jean (1928) and Edward (1932). One of these, their father destined for power.

JACK KENNEDY

Like many other dynasts, Joe Kennedy's choice fell on his first-born son. Joe jun. was to conquer Washington. However, the upbringing of all the children aimed to instil tirelessness in the pursuit of success and unwavering loyalty to family. He took an intense, though not always a kindly, interest in his offspring. While he was away he wrote to them frequently, and when he telephoned his wife, the children would line up in order of age to hear his voice. His command in his own house was absolute.

All the children were expected to compete with each other. Family sports inculcated this ethos, especially touch football. In the summers when they were not at school, Kennedy sen. ran their lives as if they were in a training-camp, even hiring a professional instructor for them. Eunice Kennedy later said of her father, 'The thing he always kept telling us was that coming in second was just no good'.

In return, the family enjoyed the benefits of its patriarch's massive fortune. While they were still children he established trust-funds for each of them, which would make all his children millionaires. Subsequent additions meant that each of his offspring started in life worth about $10,000,000. But the price to be paid for good fortune was high and the exchange not necessarily freely made. Younger Kennedys of the next two generations would have it dinned into them that they owed the Founder everything. Eunice, who survived her upbringing better than some of her siblings, remarked 'I was twenty-four before I knew I didn't have to win something every day'.

The price of failure in this family could be high. Young Jack Kennedy's health was never strong, but he felt driven to compete, especially with his much-admired elder brother: at school he once warned a date, 'Joe plays football better, Joe dances better, Joe is getting better grades'. He would spend so much time in hospitals that he later joked to a friend who planned to write his life that he should subtitle it 'A Medical History'. After his death, Bobby Kennedy commented, 'At least one-half of the days that he spent on this earth were days of intense physical pain.' In later years, when it became politically useful to project an image of glowing health, it became necessary to underplay JFK's long-running medical problems, including severe back problems (worsened or, in official accounts, caused by war injuries) and possibly Addison's disease (routinely denied in later campaigns). The success of this ploy required that JFK himself endure pain and other symptoms without self-pity or complaint. The training that enabled him to do so was administered by his father.

Young Jack had a tough time of it, forever having to compete against Joe jun., whose

natural athletic and intellectual abilities were
generally reckoned to outstrip his own. But
he was luckier than one of his sisters. Most of
the Kennedys fitted in with their father's
plans. In later years, their clan-like loyalty
to each other and to the family's advancement would be the dividend. But Rosemary
was unequal to the task. She had some slight
learning difficulties, and, perhaps because of
her condition, was prone to violent out-
bursts. Possibly her upbringing contributed
to her plight. The other Kennedys were all
taught to be aggressive; perhaps they merely
channelled it better. Kennedy sen. could not
tolerate such a daughter. Without consulting
even his wife, he had her lobotomised in
1941. She was sent to a nursing convent in
Wisconsin and her father blotted her existence from his mind.

The young Kennedy travels with his father

On the campaign trail with Franklin D. Roosevelt jun.

The Kennedys' ethical education did not figure high on the Founder's programme. Neither by precept nor by example did he teach them moral scruples. Yet his example almost certainly weighed heavily with his offspring – with his sons, especially. A flagrant philanderer himself, capable of pressing his attentions even on the women friends of his children in his own family home, his sons grew up with questionable attitudes to the opposite sex. 'Dad told all the boys to get laid as often as possible,' JFK would later explain – and if half the stories about his own exploits are to be believed, he learn the lesson. Their mother, of course, insisted on observance of the forms of Roman Catholicism, but this did not necessarily produce much practical observance of the faith's precepts, though arguably her daughters were more influenced than her sons.

At Dexter School and then at Choate and elsewhere, young Jack applied the lessons he had learned at home. He won a vote as the member of his year most likely to succeed – and demonstrated his talents by skilfully trading votes with aspirants to other accolades in order to secure the title. The vote may even have been rigged. Thus early did he start to learn how to handle elections.

As in later life, his extracurricular activities shone less brightly. One such was the Mucker's Club, so called because of the headmaster's habit of gathering all he disapproved of under this idiosyncratic term. At their nightly meetings, they would plot the subversion of the school's rigid regime. The club was discovered, and the parents of the members sent for. Kennedy sen. was displeased, but even so, when the headmaster was summoned to the telephone, wryly remarked: 'My God, my son, you sure didn't inherit your father's directness or his reputation for using bad language. If that crazy Mucker's Club had been mine, you can be sure it wouldn't have started with an "M".'

In other respects, though, Jack did follow in his father's footsteps. At seventeen, on holiday with a friend in New York, he paid his three dollars for the services offered by a brothel. A brief burst of medical anxiety in which he pestered a doctor in the middle of the night for fear of having contracted venereal disease, and the experiment was repeated.

His father had mapped out Jack's further education. In 1935 Jack accompanied his father to London, where he enrolled at the London School of Economics. Illness frustrated his plans, and he went home early. But not to recuperate – such would not be the Kennedy way. As soon as he was able, he got himself to Princeton. Illness struck again.

Finally, in the autumn of 1936, he followed his elder brother to Harvard. Joe jun. cast a long shadow, and Jack probably still felt himself caught in it.

The Founder had supported Roosevelt's Democratic Party in the election, and, by way of reward, in 1937 he was made US ambassador to England. He made a somewhat awkward figure in a Europe on the verge of war – though more awkward in retrospect than at the time – for he was both anti-Semitic and isolationist. The ambassador (as he liked to be known for the rest of his life) continued his personal direction of his son's education, pulling strings and issuing orders to send him on a study tour of Europe. Jack did it in his own reckless way, on one occasion hurtling along in his car in the Riviera at such speed that he managed to overturn it, remarking coolly to his inverted passenger, 'Well, pal, we didn't make it, did we?' The Kennedys never wanted for courage or sang-froid.

Back in Harvard, Jack put his European experiences to some use by writing a thesis on the English appeasement of Hitler. If accepted, it would enable him to graduate with honours. It was duly completed by the deadline with secretarial help courtesy of Kennedy senior. Indeed, Joe Kennedy may have been more interested in seeing it written than Jack was. He then nudged his son into turning it into a book with the help of Arthur Krock of the *New York Times*. As he explained to his son, 'You would be surprised how a book that really makes the grade with high-class people stands you in good stead for years to come.' It was not a lesson lost on young Kennedy. Over the years, he would carefully cultivate his appearance as something of an intellectual. The real extent of his intellectual capacity is still debatable. The sales of the book, however, were assured. Kennedy graduated in June. The book appeared in July; it was a best seller by September. This could have had something to do with the ambassador himself (perhaps in an overflow of paternal pride) having purchased several thousand copies.

LIEUTENANT KENNEDY

The outbreak of World War II found
Kennedy at something of a loose end. The
US did not enter the war until the end of
1941, so there was no immediate call to arms.
Equally, in the other war – the private war of
the Kennedys versus all comers – it was Joe
jun., not Jack, who was to lead the charge.
So, while his elder brother took the first steps
towards a political career in 1940, Jack
considered various possibilities with little
enthusiasm, suffered his habitual poor

health, and headed out to California for a while to continue his studies at Stanford.

As 1941 wore on, it became likely that Uncle Sam would call on its youth to put themselves on the line for liberty, democracy and the American way of life. Many obliged, among them young Jack. His health ought to have prevented him, but, in the land of equal opportunity, personal determination and a fat wallet have a way of circumventing regulations.

Jack entered the US Navy. At first, as a concession to his condition, his was a desk job with the Office of Naval Intelligence in Washington.

In his off-duty life, Kennedy continued the playboy. Typically, his response to women

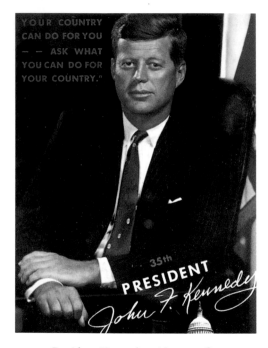

President Kennedy with part of
his inauguration speech

Rose Kennedy

seems to have been physically responsive, but emotionally remote. It is reported that, outside the sexual act itself, he did not care to be touched. Yet many women were drawn to him. Doubtless his awesome wealth was glamorous. But he also had a way of carrying his own status lightly, and a self-deprecating charm (developed, perhaps, to compensate for Joe Junior's more solid achievements), which would later prove a powerful PR weapon in politics when directed at the press corps.

One woman, however, became more important to him for a while than the rest. Inga Arvad was a journalist when Kennedy met her. She was only a few years his senior, but had already got through a couple of marriages, won praise as 'a perfect example of Nordic beauty' from Adolf Hitler, and attracted the attentions of the FBI, who had her down as a spy. For an officer in US Intelligence it was an imprudent liaison, especially since the FBI taped their pillow talk, and their discussions apparently ranged dangerously far beyond the usual 'How was it for you?' routine. It is said that the existence of these tapes, hoarded by J. Edgar Hoover, hung over Kennedy for the rest of his career.

But a figure who loomed even larger in Jack's life than Hoover was also interested in the affair. The ambassador was not much concerned at his sons imitating his philandering, but when Jack announced his intention to marry Arvad, he caused him to be reclassified as fit for active service, and so scotched the match.

After further bouts of ill health, Kennedy trained for service on PT boats. These were torpedo patrol-vessels of doubtful reliability. In January 1943, after further string-pulling, Jack got himself assigned to the South Pacific, where he would have the best chance of seeing action. There's no doubt that patriotism impelled this invalid to face the enemy. However, rivalry with Joe jun., who had recently earned his wings as a Navy pilot, may also have entered into it.

Stationed at Tulagi in the Solomons, Jack was given command of PT-109. It was a boat the world was to hear a good deal of in later years.

The Americans were trying to obstruct massive Japanese movements of men and supplies on convoys known to the Yanks as the 'Tokyo

Express'. At midnight on 1 August, the Express headed through Blackett Strait. PT boats fired on the four Japanese destroyers, themselves being picked out in spotlights for the enemy gunners. Kennedy did not participate in this action. A couple of hours later, the Express returned. PT-109 was one of three boats waiting for them. In circumstances which are now contested, the destroyer *Amagiri* rammed and sank PT-109. Kennedy supporters say he was courageously holding his position to fire on the enemy; critics, while applauding the intention, question the competence with which it was acted upon. At any event, in the small hours of 2 August, Kennedy and his crew were in the water or clinging to the wreckage. Two of them were dead.

What is not in doubt is the immense personal courage Kennedy showed over the next few days. As they swam and drifted to land, he towed one member of his crew for four hours – and this was a man whose own health was anything but robust. On making it to an atoll, Kennedy soon set out again hoping to contact a friendly vessel. Somehow managing to avoid the sharks, he swam for much of the night and returned to his men at dawn. A day later, he led them to a neighbouring island in the hope of finding provisions. Here friendly natives discovered them, and eventually they made it back to base.

His crew were warm in his praise. His commanding officer recommended him for a decoration. But it is at this point that accounts again diverge. What exactly was Kennedy being decorated for? For his conduct in the entire incident, or just for his undoubted courage in saving his crew? There was a body of informed opinion which berated him for losing PT-109 in the first place. Jack himself commented that it was a moot point whether he'd be given a medal or get thrown out over the incident – though this could reflect no more than his self-deprecating manner.

The Kennedy clan, however, entertained no such doubts. They now had a genuine hero in their midst, and, being the Kennedys, the world was going to hear about it. An unambiguously laudatory article in the *New Yorker* somehow got reprinted in the *Reader's Digest*, and would circulate in election campaigns for years to come. The story was still being recycled at Kennedy's inauguration.

John and Jackie Kennedy with their children

John Fitzgerald Kennedy

CONGRESSMAN KENNEDY

Jack spent a few more months in the Pacific before ill health sent him back home, eventually being transferred to a PT unit in Miami in the spring of 1944. Back problems continued to plague him. His exploits had done nothing for his condition, which, for the rest of his life, the Kennedys would attribute to war wounds. That summer he underwent surgery, which kept him in hospital for several weeks.

The course of his life was about to change. Joe jun. had been posted to England, where he was involved in testing a bomber which was meant to target the launching ramps for the V1 rocket bombs. He had volunteered for the mission. On 12 August he was killed in an explosion.

The repercussions spread across the Atlantic. The ambassador was hard hit by the death of his first-born and favourite son. But by Christmas his sense of destiny had sufficiently resserted itself for him to thrust the burden of his hopes onto the shoulders of his second son. In his own words, 'I told him Joe was dead and that it was therefore his responsibility to run for Congress. He didn't want to . . . But I told him he had to.'

Jack had a little while before his new career would claim his attention. He passed some of it trying to improve his health, and for a few months he worked for the newspaper mogul William Randolph Hearst, virtually as a celebrity reporter. It was all good publicity. He spent an afternoon furiously flirting with Olivia de Havilland – an encounter which ended when Jack rose to leave (having failed to make much headway) and walked straight into a cupboard.

Massachusetts was the chosen battleground (at the time of writing, Ted Kennedy is still one of the state's senators). From the first, there was no false modesty about the Kennedys' ultimate aim – in the inner circle, at least. At a family dinner, Honey Fitz toasted his grandson as the future President.

The campaign was supplied with money by the ambassador, with speeches by a PR firm, and with a quiet charm by the candidate. It was almost too quiet at first. Jack was not a natural public speaker, and seems to have found the obligation to press the flesh something of a trial. Losing one son had not made the ambassador overly tender for the well-being of his second: for months at the height of the campaign, Jack was having to get by on just three or four hours sleep a night. On one occasion after a five-mile parade, he collapsed.

The PT-109 story was much in evidence. Other voters were swayed by payments as (nominal) campaign workers. Kennedy was certainly an attractive candidate – young, heroic (with a medal to prove it), and apparently a picture of health. He was elected by an overwhelming majority.

After so strenuous a campaign, it was perhaps understandable that when Kennedy finally took up his seat in the eightieth Congress he proved less vigorous. A distaste for politics as such (at that date anyway) and continuing ill health doubtless contributed to his poor performance. Nor can it have helped that he looked so young that he could be mistaken for a lift operator or a House page. Indeed, his health was so bad that he was close enough to death on returning from a trip to Europe in 1947 to be given the last rites when the *Queen Mary* docked Stateside.

The belief that he was not long for this world may have contributed to his continuing amoral enjoyment of, and detachment from, life. He told one friend that he was living every day as if it were his last, and when one woman plucked up the courage to ask why his avoidance of relationships was matched only by his pursuit of sex, he just shrugged: 'I don't know, really. I guess I can't help it.' He looked, she recalled, 'like a little boy about to cry.'

The man who was now placed to make his voice heard in the nation's conduct of its affairs was often strangely ill-equipped to handle his own. About money he was notably vague – largely the result of never having had to bother about either spending or getting it. He had once had the odd, quasi-regal habit of seldom carrying any. He would borrow off whoever happened to be by. They, in turn, would finally learn that they had to send the IOUs direct to the ambassador. Even so, the Founder determined that 1952 would see young J.F. Kennedy enter the US Senate, and accordingly in 1951 he dispatched him on a high-profile European tour, from which Jack was meant to emerge as a plausible young statesman. This was followed by a tour of Israel and the East, in the course of which Kennedy nearly succumbed to his ailments again.

Back home, he tried to behave like a potential senator.

SENATOR KENNEDY

Never ones to shirk a fight, the Kennedys decided to put their man up against Henry Cabot Lodge, a Republican Senator and war hero who rejoiced in a 300,000 majority. Lodge made the mistake of advising Kennedy sen. not to waste his money; nothing was better calculated to inflame the patriarch's appetite for victory. The formidable Kennedy election-machine went into action. Amply oiled with funds, it was also formidably well-organized, able to pull in favours and exert influence in all manner of ways; it boasted a candidate whose actual political record could have been better, but whose remarkable qualities as a campaigner were developing; and it had a campaign organizer who was committed, effective and ruthless.

Already, something of the extraordinary Kennedy mystique was making itself felt. The family as a whole, but JFK in particular, possessed a kudos akin to a film star's. Wealth, health and looks are appealing anywhere, but in the States they are almost proof of blessedness. In addition, Jack himself came across well on TV – a factor of increasing importance in virtually all Western democracies.

By the time Lodge realized that the Kennedys were a serious threat, it was too late. Even so, the election was close-run. But in the end, in an election which generally swung the Republicans' way, Kennedy scored a significant Democratic victory.

It was no sooner gained than the strain caught up with him, and landed him in hospital.

When he took up his Senate seat in 1953 he was still fairly easy-going about his duties, though he made a number of moves towards national prominence, such as a nation-wide speaking tour of 1954. Perhaps equally important was his hiring of Theodore Sorensen. Ted Sorensen was a highly intelligent young lawyer, a liberal of wide reading and a powerful prose style. All these

The White House

Kennedy meets Harold Macmillan in London

talents were placed unreservedly at Kennedy's disposal for the next eleven years. Critics of Kennedy like to discern Sorensen's wit and flair in his employer's most celebrated and statesmanlike pronouncements. Does this matter? Most modern politicians employ speech-writers. Churchill surprised Roosevelt in this respect by writing a speech about his summit meeting with FDR on the way back across the Atlantic and having it ready to deliver on arrival. It was news to FDR that a leader could write his own speeches. But by the standards of post-war politics, Churchill was the exception rather than the rule. But just where does reasonable political team-work in support of a candidate end, and hypocrisy begin? It's hard to say. However, though Sorensen raised the tone of Kennedy's speeches and probably did much of the work for the many newspaper articles that appeared under Kennedy's name, he was not merely a brain for hire. Sorensen's personal loyalty to JFK was intense. It was more than just a job for him. Even so, in Kennedy's progress towards the presidency it is arguable that the use he made of the talents of Sorensen and others pressed beyond the boundaries of what was then usual. Whether one sees that as creditable enterprise or reprehensible deception is, to some degree, a matter of taste.

Early in his eight years as a Senator, ill health again struck. His back continued to cause intense pain, and on 21 October 1954 he underwent a risky operation to improve it. Illness dragged on for some time, extended by an infection which set in in February 1955. He was so low that one close friend felt that not only his physical, but his mental, health was at risk.

However, he showed typical spirit by turning his enforced inactivity to good account. He had earlier thought of an article about Americans who had shown courage in public life. Now, with time on his hands, the idea developed into a book. *Profiles in Courage*, as it was finally called, certainly drew upon research undertaken by Sorensen, among others. Questions have been raised as to how far it can justly be called Kennedy's book. What is beyond doubt is that it contributed greatly to his standing – especially when, in May 1957, he was awarded a Pulitzer prize for it. Kennedy was building a reputation as a thinker, and as a man of principle – something to which his cultivation of intellectuals such as John Kenneth

Galbraith also contributed. It was also a natural, if illogical, move to attribute the same moral courage of which the author wrote to the author himself, especially since he was a decorated war hero, whose wartime exploits had (so it was claimed) contributed greatly to the agony he was undergoing in hospital.

Kennedy's stock had risen high enough by the end of 1955 for him to be a serious contender for the Vice-Presidential place on the Democrat ticket at the 1956 Democratic Convention. Normally this would be a matter of winning the confidence of the Presidential candidate, who would then announce his favoured running-mate, whom the Convention would then endorse. However, Adlai Stevenson caught everyone on the hop by throwing the

Kennedy at his desk in the Oval Office

On the Kennedy yacht

nomination open to the Convention. Days (and nights) of furious canvassing ensued. Senator Kennedy and his family were, as ever, going hell for leather to win. They came close to it – very close. But as candidates fell out of the race, and after several ballots, Estes Kefauver edged ahead. In Convention and before the cameras, Kennedy was gracious in defeat. In private, he was furious. But arguably he was one of the few beneficiaries of the whole business: Stevenson and Kefauver went on to lose to Eisenhower. Kennedy had performed well, and on national TV, and had remained untarnished.

Senator Kennedy had four more years in which to prepare himself for his bid for office. He campaigned for Stevenson and Kefauver, which also had the useful effect of continuing to bring him to the notice of the nation as a whole. He undertook numberless speaking engagements. His knowledge of the network of influence – those contacts on which power often depends – was now vast. He could be vague and idealistic about policy, but when he came to electioneering he was practical and in command of detailed knowledge. He kept it up beyond the presidential election. He was riding so high that in 1958 he was re-elected to the Senate with a massive majority of over 800,000.

It was clear where he was aiming to go. His ability as a public speaker was gradually worked up to a level where it matched his personal charm. His office churned out articles, reviews and other copy over his name. He was well placed when finally, on

2 January 1960, he announced his candidacy for the Democratic Presidential nomination. What none could have known was that he had less than four years to live.

JACKIE KENNEDY

Jacqueline Bouvier was born rich, but by the time she met Kennedy in May 1952 she had fallen on comparatively hard times. The family fortunes had been hit by the Depression, and her father's principal talent when it came to money was the spending of it. Jackie's mother secured her divorce in 1940 and went on to marry another millionaire. Jackie's upbringing accustomed her to luxury, but gave no assurance of its continuance. By the time she met Jack Kennedy she was working for the *Washington Times-Herald*, and her wage was nearly all her wealth.

Not quite all: she also had invincible determination (which may have appealed to the old patriarch), and a panache and sophistication that intrigued Kennedy. She had class.

Her toughness was of most immediate use when it came to surviving the Kennedys. The family as ever lived by its own rules, and Jackie, loath to participate in their boisterous games, needed all her resilience. She confided to her sister, 'They'll kill me before I ever get to marry them.'

Jack himself was not much better. They held an engagement party in June 1952; the wedding took place in September. In between, Kennedy embarked on a trip to Europe. At the bridal dinner, Jackie jokingly read out the nearest thing to a love-letter she had received from him, a postcard from Bermuda which read 'Wish you were here, Jack'. The joke was going to wear dangerously thin.

The marriage was a lavish affair. The Archbishop of Boston celebrated the nuptial mass. The Pope sent his blessing. Jackie's father got so drunk before the ceremony that her stepfather gave her away instead. No expense was spared.

This was the style to which Jackie had every intention of becoming accustomed – to her husband's dismay. Jack had tended to be vague about money, not least because his personal finances were largely handled by his

Nikita Khrushchev

'Ich bin ein Berliner'

father's office. But he was not recklessly extravagant. Jackie, on the other hand, never tired of redecorating her various homes and buying clothes. Kennedy would set off on a trip, and come back to find the interior of their home all but unrecognizable, on one occasion protesting, 'Dammit, Jackie, why is it that the rooms in this house are never completely liveable all at the same time?'

However, such big spending was perhaps some compensation for other wrongs. Jackie played fast and loose with her husband's money; her husband played fast and loose with other women. But in the end the marriage was not balanced by mutual wrongs. It was not their respective indulgences, but their shared misfortune, that would draw them together. Jack's illness from late 1954 drew her closer to the ambassador as they both worked to sustain Jack's spirits.

The marriage was clearly under strain when Jackie suffered a miscarriage in 1956 while her husband was yachting in the Mediterranean: it took him a leisurely three days to make it back to her. Yet he was moved by the birth of his daughter Caroline in November the following year. In November 1960, when as President-elect he was busy preparing for power, he left his pregnant wife in Washington, and flew out to Palm Beach. Landing in Palm Beach, he heard Jackie had gone into premature labour, and instantly boarded a faster plane back to her side, hearing of the birth of JFK jun. in flight, rebuking himself for never being there when she needed him. However, her spending and his philandering continued unabated. Arguably, it was the death of the infant Patrick Bouvier Kennedy in 1963 that really drew them together. Tragically, they would have only a few more months to be with each other.

PRESIDENT KENNEDY

When Kennedy announced his candidacy for the Democratic nomination at the beginning of 1960 he was a strong candidate, but far from ideal. Among other things, Catholicism told against him. There had never been a Catholic President, and religion was a telling factor in US politics. His main rival, Hubert Humphrey, hoped to stop the Kennedy bandwagon in Protestant West Virginia's primary. It was a state which, according to conventional wisdom,

Kennedy could not win. But saying the word 'can't' to the Kennedys was like showing a red rag to a bull. Kennedy swiftly made explicit use of the religious card impossible for his rival, by remarking that no one was bothered about his Catholicism, or his elder brother's, when they put their lives on the line for the USA in the war. There was still a lot of ground to make up. Part of it was covered with Kennedy money; part of it with the well-practised, ruthless efficiency of the Kennedy campaign organization. But in a fight the Kennedys were not always strong on ethics. According to Judith Campbell Exner, who served as go-between, the mob also contributed to the West Virginia struggle. At any event, Kennedy won.

But come the Democratic Convention,

Kennedy had to face another opponent. In July, Lyndon B. Johnson put himself forward. He hadn't contested the primaries; but, in theory, if he could persuade the delegates, he could still be nominated. It was a long shot, but the Kennedys had put a lot of backs up. The fight was predictably hard, but Kennedy secured 806 votes to Johnson's 409.

The next question was who should be Kennedy's running mate. Much horse-trading ensued. As runner-up, Johnson might have seemed the natural choice, but it was unlikely: Johnson and Kennedy didn't seem to get on; and the all but powerless, subordinate position of Vice-President was hardly tempting to a man who, as Senate majority leader, exercised enormous influence on the Hill. And yet, in the end, LBJ

John and Jackie moments before the assassination

Lee Harvey Oswald is arrested

joined the ticket. Privately, he gave a couple of explanations to the curious. One was that the ambassador had chosen him, and over-ridden the objections of Jack and Bobby. The other was grimly prophetic: '. . . I looked it up: one out of every four Pre-sidents has died in office. I'm a gamblin' man, darlin', and this is the only chance I got.'

The Republican candidate was Vice-Presi-dent Richard Nixon. Though Kennedy cultivated an aura of intellectual liberalism, there wasn't a great deal to choose between them on policy. Jack's reputation as an author notwithstanding, Nixon's was prob-ably the more formidable mind. He deter-mined to show it to the nation in a series of four televised debates with his rival.

At the first of these Nixon was nervous, and suffered from a knee injured on his way to the studio. He had arrived early to get ready, but mostly he just got stewed up. Jack, by comparison, strolled in just before air-time. It was presentation, rather than issues, that would distinguish them. LBJ was listening in on his car radio, totting up points ('One for Nixon; one for the boy'), and he put Nixon ahead. But those who could also see the candidates got a different impression: Kennedy was handsome; Nixon's five o'clock shadow was imperfectly concealed by make-up. To millions trained by Hollywood to equate good looks with virtue, the message was clear. Kennedy henceforth had fans like a star, as well as supporters: Jackie and himself made a glamorous couple.

In the ensuing debates, advantage swung back and forth. One wit quipped that neither candidate was going to win. As it turned out, it was a close-run thing. Totting up the popular vote, Kennedy gained 49.7 per cent to his opponent's 49.6 per cent.

Kennedy was the youngest man ever to be elected President. As President-elect, he assembled around him a young Cabinet. One of his more controversial moves was to appoint his brother Bobby, who was not a lawyer, Attorney-General. The team comprised 'the brightest and the best' – or so it was claimed. But veteran Sam Rayburn was not alone in feeling some disquiet at their lack of experience. Under the US system, they were elected by no one; they were the President's appointees. As he confided to Johnson, 'Well, Lyndon, you may be right

and they may be every bit as intelligent as
you say, but I'd feel a whole lot better about
them if just one of them had run for sheriff
once.'

Millions grieved when Kennedy was killed

The JFK Memorial in Washington

THE THOUSAND DAYS

On 20 January 1961, John Fitzgerald Kennedy was sworn in as thirty-fifth President of the United States. In a freezing cold Washington, Kennedy used his inaugural address to warn his countrymen that their generation would have to fight for the freedoms they prized. He concluded by casting down a famous challenge: 'And so, my fellow Americans, ask not what your country can do for you; ask what you can do for your country.'

There are many problems in assessing exactly what JFK himself did for his country in his presidency, not least its premature conclusion. The way in which his term of office ended made him a martyr to the noble causes he had espoused – but then, what politician doesn't espouse noble causes? In the immediate wake of his death, his Thousand Days were rewritten as myth – a myth no one could well gainsay.

However, they started inauspiciously. In 1959 Fidel Castro came to power in Cuba, and soon his communist leanings became clear. Cuba is just ninety miles from US territory. In the cold war, this made it a problem. Arguably, US public opinion has been so heavily conditioned to see Cuba as a threat that, to this day, US policy towards Cuba is needlessly inflexible.

In April 1961 Kennedy seized what he hoped would be a chance to get rid of this subversive outpost in America's backyard. In some (but not enough) secrecy, he sponsored an invasion of Cuba by an army of Cuban exiles.

The Bay of Pigs invasion was a fiasco. The planning went disastrously awry, and the hapless Cubans were put ashore in a spot which denied them the chance to take refuge in the hills. Anxious to maintain the fiction that the USA had nothing to do with it, Kennedy denied them support when they needed it – though US participation was an open secret. The invasion as a whole was so open a secret that even Castro knew about it in advance. Not surprisingly, it was an inglorious failure.

The immediate political repercussions were stifled by the US people rallying round the President in a time of emergency. Nevertheless, Kennedy had not emerged well from this escapade. Anxious to recoup his position, he embarked on Operation Mongoose, which aimed covertly to topple or, better still, to kill Castro. A fair number of the CIA's dottier plots to dispose of the dictator originated in Mongoose, starting with ploys such as the shoe powder designed to make his beard fall out, and graduating to assassination. It is even said that the mob was roped in to help; it was certainly illegal enough for them, if nothing else. Perhaps fortunately for all concerned, Castro survived.

However, if Castro had merely inclined towards the Soviet bloc before, nothing could have been better calculated than the

Bay of Pigs followed by Mongoose to make Russo–Cuban alliance firm.

The Soviet Union was led by Nikita Khrushchev. Khrushchev was a wily peasant by origin, full of mischievous humour a somewhat unlikely leader of a totalitarian regime. He had some ambition to liberalize the system he ran, but was strongly opposed by factions within the USSR. But at the same time, he was ready to shore up his position with hardliners at home by taking advantage of what he took to be the new President's naïvety. Khrushchev chose to challenge Kennedy on two issues: Berlin and Cuba.

The end of World War II brought with it the end of the alliance of the USA, France and Britain with the Soviet Union. Germany was split into two, depending on which army was in occupation. East Germany fell to the Soviets. However, the Western allies had made it through to Berlin. The Western outpost in West Berlin rankled with the Soviets. They had tried to starve them out in 1948–9; the allies mounted a massive airlift to keep their half of the city supplied. Now Khrushchev thought he might try again to secure all Berlin for the communist world.

He met Kennedy in Vienna in June 1961. The Kennedys had first gone to Paris, where Jackie's welcome had been ecstatic. Though Jack had put his back out at a ceremonial planting of a tree the previous month, the couple were still the epitome of glamour. Khrushchev was not going to be so easily impressed. He had canny negotiating skills – including sudden bursts of apparent fury.

When Harold Macmillan met the President shortly afterwards, he found him somewhat dazed by his encounter. Back home he talked tough, tried to leave some route open for talks, and requested huge increases in military spending. On 13 August, the East German authorities started to partition Berlin: the infamous Berlin Wall was soon under construction.

Kennedy had to act. He sent 1,500 armed troops through East Germany along the autobahn to West Berlin. It was a calculated risk. If Khrushchev wanted war, this would be it. If not, the troops would go through and West Berlin could be further reinforced and defended. After a period of agonising tension, the troops completed their journey without incident.

The stakes were to be even higher in the next round. The US enjoyed a massive nuclear advantage over the USSR. The rationale for this was that, since the US would never launch a first strike, an adequate deterrent required sufficient weapons so that what was left after the US had been hit by the Soviets would still be enough to hit back. Even so, the imbalance was disquieting to the Russians. Khrushchev hit upon a bold plan to level the score. Under the guise of defending Cuba (which, in all fairness, was subject to the continuing hostile attentions of the US), he could turn the island into a launch pad for Soviet nuclear missiles. The greater part of the USA would be within range.

Early on 16 October 1962, Kennedy realized what was happening. In the ensuing missile crisis, the world teetered on the brink of a nuclear holocaust. He was immediately assailed by the military's demand that they be allowed to settle the matter by force. Eventually, after tense discussions in which the nerves of all at the heart of the crisis grew increasingly ragged, Kennedy opted for a blockade of Cuba. It was technically illegal, so it was termed a quarantine instead. Once it was in place, it was over to Khrushchev. If he chose to defy the US Navy, the game was up – for everybody. At 7 p.m. on Sunday, 21 October, Kennedy explained the situation to the people. Britain and France, and also the Organization of American States (not always an admirer of the US), pledged their support.

Tension rose as Soviet ships ploughed across the Atlantic. Then at 10.25 on Wednesday morning, word came that they were turning back. As Secretary of State Dean Rusk famously put it, 'We're eyeball to eyeball and I think the other fellow just blinked.'

That still left the missiles on the island. Khrushchev, now in a very difficult position at home, sent a conciliatory personal letter to Kennedy, followed up by a strident official one. On 28 October Khrushchev indicated that he would withdraw the missiles in return for a face-saving undertaking by the US never to invade Cuba, which would nominally secure the ostensible Soviet objective. In fact, a few months afterwards US Jupiter missiles in Turkey and Europe were also withdrawn, to be replaced by the Polaris submarine-based missiles.

The Cuban missile crisis was arguably Ken-

nedy's finest hour. He showed throughout a
lively sense of his responsibility to future
generations. There might have been points
which he could have managed better. But if
the worst came to the worst and the Russians
would not deal, Kennedy was in secret
preparing to make a proposal offering to
withdraw the Jupiter missiles from Turkey
in return for Soviet withdrawal from Cuba.
There would have been a high political price
to pay for this. For one whose pursuit of
office had been so single-minded, it would
have been a great sacrifice.

This was one of several signs that a new
Kennedy was emerging in the last months of
his life – a man significantly closer to the
ideal he projected. This may have something
to do with Kennedy senior's stroke at the
end of 1961, which left the patriarch alert,

but, to his frustration and fury, unable to communicate normally. If Kennedy hadn't already broken from his father's influence, perhaps he did then.

In domestic policy he was well disposed towards the civil-rights movement, though arguably not a passionate supporter of it. His administration's caution might be ascribed to pragmatism, or to the nobler motive of seeking to sustain the social order in the South while extirpating racism. However, his pace and methods frustrated even a comparatively moderate black-leader like Martin Luther King. Arguably, it was black militancy that drove Kennedy to take a firmer, more moral stand.

There's no way of knowing how his policy would finally have developed in SE Asia. He backed Diem's South Vietnamese regime with military advisers, but declined to send in the regular troops. It's impossible to know whether he would have saved the USA from defeat and humiliation.

A more plausible case for his success can be made from the continuing story of US-Soviet relations, in which he continued to deploy a mixture of toughness (including going to West Berlin and famously pledging the West to its defence with the words 'Ich bin ein Berliner') and conciliation designed to secure limits to each side's armaments. Given the intense anti-communist feeling of the US electorate, this was an especially difficult and creditable endeavour.

In his private life, many reports suggest that he was as dissolute as ever – possibly dependent on 'speed', courtesy of Dr Jacobson, and certainly sexually promiscuous. Yet as noted, there were also signs of greater closeness between Jackie and himself towards the end. That, indeed, was why she was with him in Dallas in November 1963 as he campaigned for his re-election in 1964.

The immediate reaction of almost everyone in the wake of the assassination of 22 November was that it must be part of some larger plot. How could an event of such significance be caused by the whim of a lone man of doubtful mental stability? Many have continued to cling to conspiracy theories of one kind or another. Kennedy certainly had enemies. Dallas as a whole was hostile to him. Could it be the Soviets, the Mob, even some branch of government itself? Lee Harvey Oswald never lived to explain his actions, for he was gunned down himself by Jack Ruby while in police custody. The whole business began to look like the blackest farce.

Whatever the real reason for his death, the manner in which his family responded to it is beyond dispute. In the immediate aftermath of the shooting, Mrs Kennedy remained with her husband's mutilated body. At the funeral on the 25th, she appeared a figure of sombre elegance with her two young children, and hearts all round the world went out to the family and the nation in their grief.

LIFE AND TIMES

Julius Caesar
Hitler
Monet
Van Gogh
Beethoven
Mozart
Mother Teresa
Florence Nightingale
Anne Frank
Napoleon

LIFE AND TIMES

JFK
Martin Luther King
Marco Polo
Christopher Columbus
Stalin
William Shakespeare
Oscar Wilde
Castro
Gandhi
Einstein

FURTHER MINI SERIES
INCLUDE

ILLUSTRATED POETS

Robert Burns
Shakespeare
Oscar Wilde
Emily Dickinson
Christina Rossetti
Shakespeare's Love Sonnets

FURTHER MINI SERIES
INCLUDE

HEROES OF THE WILD WEST

General Custer
Butch Cassidy and the Sundance Kid
Billy the Kid
Annie Oakley
Buffalo Bill
Geronimo
Wyatt Earp
Doc Holliday
Sitting Bull
Jesse James